John,

Hope you like the

Book —

Joe Kochis

Horns, Guns and Hunters

———

Joe Kochis

ISBN 0-9669300-0-2

Printed by
Maverick Publications
Bend, Oregon

TABLE OF
CONTENTS

I hope that you enjoy reading the following poems as much as I enjoyed writing them. Many of the central ideas came from experiences I've had throughout my life and gave me the chance to relive them again. Certainly not all of the poems are a part of my personal experience, but, a little imagination thrown in now and then tends to make things more interesting.

I would like to thank the people that encouraged me to continue this endeavor, and also, a special thanks to Jill Freeman of Philomath, Ore. who drew the illustrations in the book.

Those of us that have had the opportunity to enjoy hunting know that bringing home game is only a fraction of a successful trip. The chance to be with friends without the rigors of life's daily pressures is something in which to look forward when the days start to cool and the leaves change colors. Good reading, good hunting!

Every year before opening day, we either make individual bets or put money in a pool on who will get the biggest buck. This particular year my hunt took me to a private ranch in Idaho where I thought my chances of getting a record set of antlers was something better that 100%. I, therefore, made a bet with a friend that was hunting our "old" territory in the upper breaks of the John Day river east of Shaniko, Oregon. The following poem accompanied the amount of the bet in an envelope to my friend.

THE HUNT

The bet was made as is done each year,
which hunter would come home with the biggest deer.
"The size of the rack is what we'll judge em' by."
"We'll use a tape to deter any lie."

The pact was made, with money on the line,
to hunt down our bucks in limited time.
The vow I made to all that could hear,
that I would come home with the rack of the year.

Patience and stealth is what I would require,
to tell the big story as we would sit by the fire.
The bucks that I saw were not huge in size,
and none met the vision that I had in my eyes.

Day after day I hunted hither and yon,
I began to think that the big buck was gone.
The last day arrived I knew I had to score,
the creeping thoughts I had shook me to the core.

The dreams of a giant may not be mine this year
and I would have to settle for a smaller deer.
Then out on the slope the big guy appeared,
I knew this was the one, the king of all deer.

The distance was long, my gun measured up to the task,
I would have that big buck, at last, at last.
Through the scope the horns didn't look that fantastic,
but it was too late my brain was on automatic.

After the crack of the rifle and an eternity of time,
the buck tumbled down to rest by a pine.
As I approached the deer I could see that my "prize,"
did not meet my vision of large antler size.

My pride was destroyed I could hardly speak,
this was the smallest buck that I had seen all week.
Not one to give up quite so fast,
I began to think of a good story at last.

"Them horns ain't big," we compared by the looks,
but by damn that shot was one for the books.

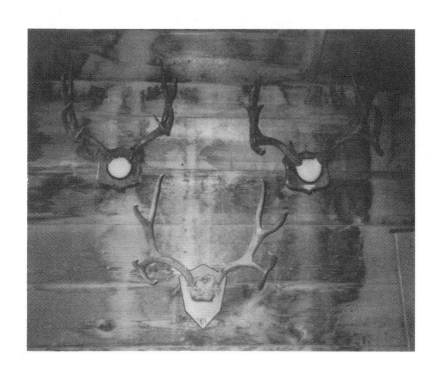

Most of us that have done a lot of hunting over the years have had the opportunity to hunt with at least one individual whose character stood out light-years ahead of most men. They are the true leaders that get things done without fanfare and quietly charge ahead day after day. Giving up or quitting is not part of their vocabulary, and when a new obstacle is placed in their path, the only way they know is to meet the challenge head-on. You will find that this is a battle of will between two very strong individuals, the elk and the man.

THE CHALLENGE

Their spirits were one of blood and steel
they had fought and won through strength and zeal.
The man was known for his triumphs of the past,
the elk known only for his ability to outlast.
Their paths had crossed throughout the years,
during the season of taking, during the season of fear.

He knew it was the last of the hunts he would make,
his body endured more than his heart could take.
He sat on his "stand" in the wet and the cold,
his senses had diminished from getting old.

The elk had lost in this very last fight,
driven from the herd into the cold of the night.
The wounds of the battle had taken it's toll,
weakened his spirit, weakened his soul.

They both thought of a time when their energy would fail,
and they would no longer fight for the "holy grail."
Fate drew them near in the deep of the year,
during the season of taking, during the season of fear.

The lead gray sky with swirling snow and dread,
was like a dance of evil for the future dead.
The two unaware of their time to come,
in this cold gray place of clouds and no sun.
He sat there waiting for his prey to arrive,
his body was freezing and barely alive.
His mind was drifting from the hunt at hand,
like the snow of the winter across the barren land.

The elk sensed a presence of fear and death,
as he circled the "stand" slowly, and ran short of breath.
This was his home of yesterday's past,
where life was forever and would last and last.

The man had entered his sacred place,
he would meet this last challenge face to face.
The man saw the blur of the movement ahead,
and knew that the challenge was to kill or be dead.

The charge of the elk, the explosion from the gun,
was their last act of aggression in this land of no sun.
Both had died in the heat of the fight,
their spirits and souls had since taken flight.
In life they met the challenge to command the top of the hill,
In death they had fought with strength and steel will.
They would not have it different these two sons of the land,
they defended their beliefs, the elk and the man.
Fate drew them together in the fall of the year,
during the season of taking, during the season of fear.

Every hunter should have the opportunity to have at least one horse in their hunting life like Lucky. He stands about thirteen hands maximum, and possibly weights 950 pounds. I've put him into places where no horse should go, due to a lack of good sense on my part, and never had a wreck. Some of the territory we hunt in has a lot of space between good places to hunt and camp; therefore, Lucky got a new assistant.

LUCKY'S NEW FRIEND

It's that time of year when the hunt draws near,
the cool of the weather the packing of gear.
I stay in the pasture most of the time,
but when deer season comes my heart starts to climb.

We'll be walking the ridges and looking for deer,
me and my rider, a special time of year.
The day arrives to pack up for our stay,
they were loading the guns, saddle, ropes and hay.

It wouldn't be long before my rider would arrive,
to load me in the trailer for a three hour ride.
He finally come to get me and hooked the rope to my halter,
I jumped into the trailer and my heart started to falter.

Before my eyes in the space up ahead,
stood a Honda 4-wheeler smelling of gas and bright red.
I had been put aside into second place,
my thoughts in my mind started to race.

No longer would I be the one he would ride,
my master had destroyed my heart and my pride.
We parked in the place where we usually do,
they unloaded me and that 4-wheeler too.

They put us together me and that machine,
I took a look around and started to get mean.
My leg cocked back like the hammer of a gun,
I would kick this bastard half way to the sun.

When I turned it loose you could feel the jar,
but the sound and the fury went a little too far.
My master rushed to see what was going on,
I just stood there looking like nothing was wrong.

He took the machine to a separate place,
where I couldn't plant my foot in it's rear or it's face.
The following days I stood alone in the corral,
my master rode the machine, my heart really fell.

Then the day came when I thought it was all done,
my rider came to me with saddle and gun.
But he spoke of the buck way over a rim,
where 4-wheelin' stops and horse ridin' begins.

My ears perked up with these words of joy,
he thought there was life left in this old boy!
We rode out of camp to that place on the rim,
as I looked down I knew my work would begin.

It was steep with rocks, brush and no trail,
I'd been through this before and I would not fail.
We went into the valley far, far below,
the going was rough and very, very slow.

The deer lay there on a very steep slope,
me and my rider, saddle, gun and rope.
I braced myself to get the deer on my back,
legs tied to the cinch saddle straps held his rack.

We headed up the hill through rocks and brush,
the steepness of the climb gave my heart a rush.
As we neared the top, my master pulling on my halter,
I could feel my legs begin to falter.

For at the top was eight miles more I feared,
to pack this load of saddle, rifle and deer.
I would never give up with my rider by my side,
It was something deep within me, my strength and my pride.

When we arrived at the top, my rider and me,
was something I thought I never would see.
Out on the flat was the wife of the rider,
with that darn 4-wheeler sittin' there beside her.

I was tired and I'd had enough
and all I wanted was to unload this stuff.
The machine took the burden of my pack,
left me and my rider for the eight miles back.

We took our time traveling and enjoyed the ride,
I had done my job and restored my pride.
We rode into camp my rider and me,
I pranced a little so that 4-wheeler could see.

But when the lights went out and in the dark of night,
the horse walked to the 4-wheeler but not for a fight.

I was glad to see you on that hill today,
if you were a horse I would share my hay.
But just remember when it really gets rough,
this old horse is still very, very tough.

Looks like you'll be here for years, it seems,
I think you and I will make a hell of a team.

Deep In the night the rider will remember,
when he saw his old horse nuzzle the 4-wheeler's fender.

At one time or another we have all been guilty of "holding out" on our hunting partners after seeing a big buck or a big bull, in hopes of getting a second chance to bag it for ourselves. This is one of those stories, only, with a little different twist.

THE BONNER RIDGE KID

The Bonner Ridge Kid was young and lean,
he hunted with great skills, his senses were keen.
He'd killed elk with a gun in the years past,
but needed a new method to make the hunt last.

He felt that his skills were going to waste
and he wanted a challenge face to face.
So he took up the bow with "camo" and gear,
and sat out to find the "bull of the year."

The rumor spread that a big bull was near,
the "kid" set his mind to outdo his peers.
He found it's tracks in the valley below,
he shouldered his quiver, arrows and bow.

Stalking the bull day after day,
put his mind to the test to conquer his prey.
But the elk was wise and kept out of range,
and that's' when the kid started to act a little strange.

Later in the year the men of the chase,
joined the kid to find the big bull's place.
They noticed a difference in the kids attitude,
rather than to help he tried to elude.

When they said here, he said there,
he tried to head them away from the bull's lair.
At the end of the season nobody would score,
the kid secretly grinned, he'd hunt the bull once more.

But, the men of the hunt had a different plan,
they devised a trick to play on this young man.
They called a hunter, not from their clan,
to say that he'd killed the "bull of the land."

"Twas a giant," he claimed, "a rack for the books,"
when the kid heard the story he wanted to look.
But the hunter was wise beyond the kids years,
he conjured a tale just for the kid's ears.

"I'm sorry," he said, "the elk rack is gone,"
I shipped it off to be mounted, the time will be long."
"But I can tell you a story you'll never forget,
I dropped that big bull by the "stand" where you sat."

The kid couldn't believe what his ears had been told,
but deep in his heart the truth had struck cold.
It was hard to bear the loss that he felt,
very hard to believe the fate he'd been dealt.

He mopped around for months it seemed,
as if he couldn't shake a very bad dream.
Then a man from the hunt said "we'll help if we can,
to find another "bull of the land."

"But you help us too if we're on his trail,
because like you, we don't like to fail."
The kid really listened, took the words to heart,
"next year, he thought, I'll make a fresh start."

There are some things, that evoke a lot of memories and emotion for any hunter. I can't imagine anything more, than the hunting rifle that belonged to your dad. This next poem is not only about dad's favorite rifle, it's about the great person that took him out elk hunting day after day. Rain, snow or sun Bill would have dad up at 5:00AM every day of the season. I would sometime get a chance to hunt during a weekend of the season with them. Pop would complain a bit, after all he was in his eighties, however, at daylight he would be out there with the best of them. I truly believe that Bill contributed a great amount in extending my fathers life just by keeping him interested in looking forward to the next day.

TO BILL

The first time I saw it was in '52,
the stock was walnut the barrel deep blue.
It was a .308 Winchester with a velvet bolt action,
would meet the requirements of any hunter's satisfaction.

The owner would show it with limited pride,
he didn't express the great feeling that he kept inside.
He mounted a peep site to this beautiful gun,
knew that it would well serve him for years to come.

They worked together as if they were a team,
the hunter and his rifle, like a well oiled machine.
Over the years the gun served him well,
when he squeezed the trigger the deer and elk fell.

Then came a time when the vision would blur,
a scope was added to make the shot sure.
Like the rebirth of youth his confidence did rise,
he could hit anything that he saw with his eyes.

They became a legend in the years to come,
the hunter with his skill and the .308 gun.
No shot was too far for his eyes to seek,
no distance too long for the gun to reach.

Life had taken us apart throughout the years,
but we still got together to hunt elk and deer.
I looked at the gun that had served him so long,
the blue on the barrel had long since gone.

They were two of a kind this man and his gun,
they had risen to the challenge, they had tried and won.
The ravages of time took the hunter's life away,
but the old .308 Winchester wanted to stay.

The gun went to the hunter's friend with a note on the stock,
saying, "my previous owner liked to hunt a lot."
"If it's not too much to ask of this scarred up old gun,
in the fall of the year take me out for my fun."

"I'll serve you well if you take care of me,
and I'll hit anything that my sights can see."
"We cannot replace the days that we had in past years,
but we can still have a good time by hunting elk and deer."

You were first in line to have this gun,
'cause you helped the old hunter have his fun.
He spoke of you in the highest regard,
as we talked of hunting out back in the yard.

We'll remember those times with the hunter and his gun,
they were the best of the years, the greatest of fun.
If in telling this story it seems a little sad,
the .308 Winchester, it belonged to my dad.

Now maybe we don't like to admit it, but, most of us get a little bit of help when it comes to preparing for a hunting trip. I have to admit, I'm probably the most spoiled hunter in the country. My wife doesn't take care of the rifle, shells, horses and tack, but just about everything else. I tried to capture her thoughts during one of those times.

THE HUNTER'S WIFE

She watched from the kitchen in the early morning light,
his walk was different his demeanor more bright.
She had seen this repeated year after year,
it comes with change in the weather, when frost is near.
It was time to find things he would usually forget,
call it to his attention—"did you think of that yet."
She smiled at his behavior like the excitement of a child,
his voice was louder and his eyes a little wild.

She finished the dishes and after making the bed,
found his old pants and his shirt that was red.
She collected all the clothes that he would need to pack,
and put them in the room that had his gun in a rack.
A list was made of the food he would take,
then she went to the store; maybe she'd even bake a cake.
She had done this so often she knew what to cook,
and he would let her know how good it was, with a special
      look.
She thought to herself, "why do I do all of this,
it's not our first years of marital bliss."
She would get a little mad at things he would want her to do,
after getting all of his clothes, he'd ask, "honey where's my
      shoes."

There would be a flurry of activity in the days ahead,
he'd collect all of his gear and put it in the pickup bed.
He'd hook up the trailer to carry his old horse,
put hay and oats in to feed him of course.

The day arrived when he'd be gone for a while,
they parted with a kiss, a hug and a smile.
As he drove down the lane toward his quest of the year,
she thought, "is all of this worth it, to hunt a damn deer?"

After the hunting seasons are over and it's too early to start planning for the next year, we usually have a "get-together" to explain the finer points of hunting, just in case we forgot something during our trip. Talk about cutting straight to the chase, this bunch is something to behold.

AFTER THOUGHTS

The men of the hunt, the men of the hunt,
they show off their rifles and speak very blunt.
They gather together late in the year,
to tell their stories and drink a little beer.

Exploits are told to the n'th degree,
embellished with beer and pictures to see.
"Look at that buck," with photo in hand,
"it's the biggest deer ever to come from this land.

A booming voice from the back of the room,
says,"you were five feet away and your camera on zoom."
They laughed and cheered at this bit of jest,
"another round of beer, you haven't heard the rest."

Another got up to tell all that could hear,
how he tracked over rocks to find his deer.
There were no prints to be found, so he did tell,
he got on all fours and started to smell.

He crawled for miles following the scent,
and finally caught up where the animal went.
The last few yards with stealth he did creep.
Jumped up to shoot, only to find a sheep.

They laughed 'till they cried tears spilling from their eyes,
"lets drink some more beer and tell some more lies."
The stories went on for hours it seemed,
then the last man got up as if in a dream.

"As you all know my gun is not large,
and a long shot for it is one hundred yards."
"But I saw this buck way up on the hill,
'twas a thousand yards away but standing still."

"I thought of a plan to shoot this deer,"
his eyes looked around and he took a drink of beer.
"The bullet from the gun would not go that distance,
"some way I would have to give it assistance."

"Then it came to me in the light of day,
how this was very similar to a football play."
"Like a guard on the line breaking open a hole,
so the man with the ball has a clear run at the goal."

"I took two fast shots, the first to break the resistance,
the one right behind, would travel the distance."
I have proof of what I say,
the deers' in the locker on this very day."
"So if you boys need some help in sighting your gun,
don't pay an expert, I'll do it for fun."

It was quiet for a moment for the story to sink in,
then the speaker looked around and started to grin.
It started like a wave coming from the sea,
the roar of the laughter, the looks of glee.
They laughed and drank to the break of dawn,
and hoped that this night would live on and on.

The men of the hunt, the men of the hunt,
they show off their rifles and speak very blunt.
They gather together late in the year,
to tell their stories and drink a little beer.

When you're young, you think you can accomplish just about anything. I thought I could train and ride just about anything that walked on four feet. Surprising how wrong you can be. If Lucky was the best of horses in the brush, this next horse shouldn't have been born. As Lucky belonged to the whiskey and beer bunch, the horse in this next poem should have stayed with the tea and white wine set.

HORSIN' AROUND

I had bought this horse for huntin' trips
he was long in the neck and narrow at the hips.
Stood sixteen hands high with spindly legs,
nothin' to be proud of about nothin' to brag.

I trained him to pack the schooling was brief,
he would spook from his shadow and trip over a leaf.
Even though his temperament was just a little tough,
I thought he would make it when the going got rough.

Then the day came to load up for the ride,
I had a horse rack on the pickup, to that he was tied.
We headed for the Steens in southeast corner of the state,
where this horse was to meet a very strange fate.

Upon our arrival we loaded up our gear,
the horses were decked out from their tails to their ears.
I packed all the grub on this homely thing,
pack bags were full, to his sides they did cling.

I suspected a problem when we put on the pack,
he jumped four feet sideways when it hit his back.
It was like a whole new world to this giraffe of a horse,
it was obvious his schoolin' wouldn't last the course.

We had four miles of steep trails and brush,
through creek beds and rocks the water would rush,
It wasn't much of a challenge to the horse up ahead,
his name was Lucky and he was damn well bred.

But we set out on our trek of hunting the deer,
come hell or high water we would persevere.
We headed up the hill there was snow in the air,
but we were young and tough and didn't much care.

Two miles up the grade where it was straight up and down,
I was leadin' the giraffe when his hind legs broke ground.
His back feet were down on the low side of the trail,
I pulled hard on his halter to no avail.

Instead of driving with his feet to get back in stride,
he sucked them under and tumbled down the side.
He rolled end over end 'till he hit the creek,
where his head should be all I saw was feet.

His head was stuck between two rocks,
one nostril suckin' water, the other blowin' snot.
One hind leg was hung on a low leanin' limb,
his chances of survival was lookin' mighty slim.

But I cut off the pack and chopped out a trail,
just in case this bastard could shake a tail.
I untangled his legs and jerked on his head,
he was moanin' and groanin' and his eyes were red.

He finally got up and he saw the new trail,
I was leadin' this horse and had to run like hell.
We jumped across the creek to the other side,
I was determined the pack bags on his back they would ride.

My new propane stove was smashed a little flat,
the eggs, bacon and bread was jumbled up in the pack.
My temper ran short in this rocky creek bed,
and I thought maybe this horse would be better off dead.

Common sense overcome my anger again,
I loaded up the pack and I was determined to win.
We arrived at our camp and hunted for awhile,
limited out on our deer and were coming back in style.

I packed him light for the returning ride,
the other horse shouldered his burden with pride.
My friend led the horse on the down hill trek,
when we arrived at the place where he had his wreck.

Like a bolt of lightening he exploded from the back,
knocked my friend face down and was laying very flat.
I grabbed the halter rope as he started to go past,
he was hell bent for leather and going very fast.

After everything calmed down I turned to my friend,
and said "are you OK, are you ready to go again."
He looked at me with mud on his face,
said that horse jumped over him and didn't leave a trace.

We thought we had it made the rest of the way to the truck
one horse lightly loaded the other with our bucks.
When we arrived at the place where our journey began,
after unpacking the horses, old ""giraffe" acted up again.

The other horse jumped in as good as you please,
but ring-ding wouldn't go, I was pleading on my knees.
Then there comes a time when it's do or die,
I'd leave him layin' in the desert and for the buzzards in the
sky.

With my gun in my hand I led him to a tree,
he was destined for hell at the count of three.
Just short of the time when my finger pulled the trigger,
the eyes on that horse got bigger and bigger.

I saw a change come over this equestrian charge,
his temperament had changed even though his eyes were large.
We walked to the truck he was like a feather in my hand,
he had become the best horse to ever walk the land.

After the end of our trip the horse was up for sale,
I knew that his memory of the hunt would pale.
He went to a family in a new location,
where their daughter was good at the art of equitation.

A couple of years later and to my surprise,
the horse and his rider had taken first prize,
You just never know when you drag yourself up from the mud,
that you may have been stomped by a horse of good blood.

Somewhere back in time, during the early years of our country, the trappers that came West used a lot of landmarks to keep from getting lost. Even with their keen sense of direction, helped along with a good memory, they would occasionally get "turned around" for three or four days. We've all been there, done that. This next poem is about one of those occasions.

THE ART OF GETTING LOST

Walker, oh Walker where have your been,
we found you once now you're lost again.
We followed your tracks through desert and snow,
but lost them for good west of Shaniko.

We all tried hard to get his directions straightened out,
even gave him a compass, he'd watch the arrow turn about.
When it came time to return for the day,
he just couldn't believe what the compass would say.

A fool proof method was devised after all,
we gave him some string in a great big ball.
"Just tie one end to camp when you leave at daylight,
and roll it back in a ball when returning at night"

This worked pretty good the first time or two,
but something went wrong, it came out of the blue.
The string broke from camp as he started out for the day,
we found the end of it five miles away.

The string went down in the canyon below,
then back on the ridge it went to and fro'.
Just when we thought we'd neared the end of it's course,
the string side-hilled downward, back and forth.

Like a giant spider Walker had woven a web,
he was looking for camp where he'd tied the string to his bed.
We were hopelessly tangled in this sorry mess,
this idea was wrong we had to confess.

We went back to camp and headed for home,
never could find where Walker did roam.
Winter, spring and summer we looked all around,
but to no avail, Walker couldn't be found.

That very next fall we camped in the same place,
we thought of our friend that didn't leave a trace.
Then from the East we heard someone holler,
we all looked around and, by God, it was Walker!

We ask where he'd been for such a long time,
he was lookin' good and said he was feelin' fine.
He told lots of stories he'd had lots of fun,
when he was lost a man told him, to follow the sun.

Then he gave out mementos that he had in his pack,
they laid out a trail of his long route back.
There were trinkets from China, a little Russian bear,
scarves made in France for the women to wear.

Walker said he didn't know exactly were he'd been,
didn't think he was ready to take the trip again.
He said this year, for him, we wouldn't have to look,
he would just hang around here and be the camp cook.

Looking back over all of the years of hunting, the place we used to stay in the Steens Mountains in Southeast Oregon was probably the most memorable. You had to be young to appreciate and enjoy such a place.

HOTEL D'STEENS

There's a place back in time where we used to go,
the hillsides were steep and the water ran cold.
Little Indian Creek was the waterway,
about halfway up was a great place to stay.

It was built by a Basque who used to herd sheep,
the log sides were aspen the roof was steep.
It sat on that flat for around fifty years,
had long since been abandoned by the Basque and his peers.

But when your roughin' it out on a huntin' trip,
this looked better than any luxury ship.
We would arrive there early and to no one we would tell,
so that we could take possession of our high class hotel.

It was fourteen feet long and twelve foot wide,
the floor was dirt, a bit Spartan inside.
The door was short and the hinge broken on top,
when it opened to the inside it scraped a lot.

The roof on the left side was all still there,
but the part on the right was nothin' but air.
The spaces between the logs that had been filled long ago,
provided us with air conditioning when the wind did blow.

We would spread out our sleeping bags way in the back,
put our grub in the front along with our tack.
To the right of the door we'd build a fire place,
so the smoke from our fire would escape into space.

This was living at its best, our home away from home,
we'd watch the stars at night out of our open air dome.
When it was blowin' snow and the skies looked like lead,
the horse blankets and tarps would cover our beds.

We'd rise before daylight to cook eggs and bacon,
our hands cold as hell and legs still shakin'.
After moving around and getting something to eat,
the feeling would return to our hand and feet.

Lunches were packed and we would shoulder our guns,
we'd be at the top of the mountain before the rising sun.
After hunting all day and a long walk back,
it was good to return to that log cabin on the flat.

But after four to five day in this humble little place,
my partner and I started to run out of space.
We never changed clothes and we couldn't take a shower,
The aroma inside begin to have a hell of a lot of power.

We would load our packs and, if lucky, our deer,
and say goodby to our cabin of once-a-year.
On our trek down the hill from that quaint little place,
I would think of home and quicken the pace.

You wait all year for the first day of deer season. The anticipation is practically as exciting as the hunt. By the time your ready to start out on opening morning, your nerves are on razor edge and you know, for sure, that this is going to be the day. But, even the best of premonitions can be changed by something as simple as a sunrise. I left out a picture that would illustrate this poem simply because I didn't have one exactly as described in the poem. I leave it up to your imagination as the reader to come up with your own picture.

OPENING DAY

It was opening day of the season before daylight,
the air was crisp and the feeling was right.
After gathering his gear to hunt for the day,
he headed out of camp his flashlight lit the way.
He hiked down the ridge, took the left-hand spur
found a likely spot that would hide him for sure.
He settled down by a juniper tree,
looked across the canyon and took in what he could see.

To his right down the ridge on the opposite side,
was a small stand of aspen, a good place for a buck to hide.
Up the hill to his left about four hundred yards,
was an out crop of rocks that ended, in a rim quite large.
Directly in front and all across the hillside,
was short sagebrush where nothing could hide.
In the bottom of the canyon was a small rock wall
that followed the creek down to a water fall.
It was a perfect place to see a big buck,
and he was sure that he would with a little bit of luck.
He could picture him now moving up toward the rim,
the hunter was ready and anxious for the day to begin.

The rays from the sun turned the rim light red,
made a badger start to stir from his rocky bed.
The aspens in the shade gave off their own light,
the leaves were yellow and extremely bright.
And colors in the clouds on the horizon in the west,
this was like a landscape painting by God's very best.
The hunter was in awe at the sight he could see,
but the clinking sound of a rock took him from his reverie.

He moved his eyes without turning his head,
if the sound was made by a buck, he would soon be dead.
He looked across from where the sound had come,
it was down in the shade and out of the sun.

He scanned everything above and below,
then the whole hillside moved as a breeze began to blow.
The constant watching in the cold morning air,
made his eyes begin to water as he continued to stare.
He wiped them clear with a handkerchief in his hand,
and then once more began to look at the land.

* * *

The buck had watched from the aspen patch,
he had eaten all night and wanted to get back.
His bed was around on the back side of the rim,
he had to cross the hillside so he had better begin.
The scent of something new had invaded this place,
he listened for sounds but didn't hear a trace.
He had watched for an hour for any movement up ahead,
only to find quiet hillsides instead.

His head was down so his horns wouldn't show,
he would take two steps and stop his movements were slow.
Caution and stealth had kept him here,
he would never panic, or be overcome by fear.
He was halfway across when he made the sound,
he had kicked a rock loose and it rolled across the ground,
It went down and behind him and hit the rock wall,
it clinked pretty loud when another rock stopped its fall.
He froze in his tracks with his head to the ground,
he looked and listened for any movement or sound.

It was up to his left under a juniper tree,
it didn't move around but it was different to see.
He hadn't seen it before when he was in the aspen patch,
but he knew all it could see was the top of his back.
Then a breeze came up to his relief,
his stay on this open hillside would be fairly brief.
Like a ghost in the night he glided up in a rush,
his movements were camouflaged by wind on the brush.

He stopped once more to check his course up ahead,
and allowed himself to slowly turn his head.
He saw a movement of white by the juniper tree,
and now he knew it was a man that he could see.
He was a short distance from the top of the hill,
where the wind had stopped and again was still.
Time was running short for the sun would soon be here,
and would expose the giant rack and body of the deer.
He wanted to run but the distance was too great,
and any fast movement may seal his fate.
Again he would move a step or two up the hill,
and continued to sneak slowly, against his will.

At the edge of the sunlight but in the shade still,
was twenty yards to safety and to get over the hill.
He knew he had to run with all of his might,
before the hunter had a chance react to his flight.
He exploded from the shade and went around the rim,
the return to a safe haven was his again.

* * *

The hunter looked up as he heard the sound up the slope.
and shouldered his rifle to look through his scope.
The white of it's rump was all he could see,
as the buck jumped out of sight in it's attempt to flee.
He put his gun down and took an apple from his pack,
and thought, "it must have been a doe, I didn't see any rack."
Then he returned to his gaze and what he saw was grand,
the excitement of the chase, the beauty of the land.
Hunting was great, but there was much, much more,
he knew he had just looked through heaven's front door.

Every young man has his dreams about meeting the perfect girl in the perfect setting. In the following poem, a young cowboy takes a few days off for hunting and, at first, it looked as if his dreams had come true. However—

ENCOUNTER

It had been a long hard year for the horse and the man,
and he was looking forward to the hunt the land.
He had wrangled cattle all summer long,
now that fall was here his worries were gone.
That old line shack back up on the mountain,
was a good spot to be for deer and elk scoutin'.
He loaded his gear on the pinto pack horse,
and rode out from the ranch up the long steep course.
The horse he was riding was a pretty good one,
Then there was Rusty the dog, a mean son-of-a-gun.
On the way up the hill he started to think back,
he had done this many times and that was a fact.
A lot of years had past since his first cattle ride,
being by himself all this time made him lonely inside.
He was twenty eight and all he had done,
was to look for cows in the rain, snow and sun.
There must be more than to live this kind of life,
he thought of having his own place, and maybe a wife.

He arrived at the place and put his gear in the shack,
turned the horses loose in the corral out back.
After gathering some wood and taking it inside,
he looked at his temporary home with a sense of pride.
There was a stove in one corner opposite the door,
a bunk to the right and a cow hide on the floor.
Four sets of deer horns, that were nailed to the walls,
told stories of success while hunting in the fall.
He hung up his gun, put his bullets on a shelf,
the dog chewed a stick by the stove to amuse himself.

He liked this old shack with it's bleached out boards,
and it's spectacular view that overlooked the gorge.
He sat on the steps and took in the scene,
it was like a landscape painting right out of a dream.

The wind picked up there was a chill in the air,
fall had come early to his high mountain lair.
He knew this experience was a gift of God's best,
and was reserved for people that lived in the West.

His spell was broken by a movement on the hill,
a stranger come toward him against his will.
"Who could this be invading my place,"
he said to himself with a grimace on his face.
But a second glance put his mind in a whirl,
this was the walk of a genuine girl!
She was no ordinary hiker he determined at fifty yards,
she wore little laced-up boots and black leotards.
The pack she had on was half her size,
she had short blond hair and dark brown eyes.
"My God," he thought, " can this be real,"
his emotions were on edge and hard to conceal.
He said, "sit yourself down and pull off that pack,
looks like you've got a hell of a load on your back."
She concurred with his request and dropped her gear,
and took a seat beside him, he was shakin' with fear.
"She will probably leave if I don't act right,
but if I say nothing she'll think I'm not very bright."
"Well, he said, "what do you think of the view,"
she turned and said, "I like it too."
He looked at those eyes and knew this was it,
she was the woman of his dreams, here where he sit.
They talked until the sun went behind the hill,
and the wind died down and the night grew still.

His mind raced ahead as he asked her inside,
he was afraid of failure and wounding his pride.
But to his surprise she said "OK",
"it's been a terribly long hike and a very cold day."
"And if it's the same to you and if it's all right,
I'd like to stay right here for the rest of the night."

He skipped up the steps and opened the door,
shook his head in disbelief once more.
She glided up behind him with graceful strides,
she entered the doorway and looked inside.

The world exploded like a huge fire ball,
she said, "what is that there hanging on the wall."
He looked at her with a little bit of fear,
and said, "that's my gun for huntin' deer."
She come totally unglued like a broom tailed bronc,
she was flailin' around like "gators" in a swamp.
She was yellin' about him killin' our animal friends,
and called him a murderer over and over again.
His heart dropped down at the words she used,
he couldn't speak he was very confused.
His old dog Rusty that never run from a fight,
was headin' for the door in a jet-like flight.

He was trying to think of something he could do,
then it dawned on him like a shot from the blue.
He dug in his gear and pulled a bottle out,
it was eighty-six proof and pretty damn stout.
He said, "take a drink of this, its barley and corn,
something you can use and nothing you will scorn."
She stopped and grabbed the bottle from his hand,
and belted down a swig like a drinkin' man.

But to no avail she continued on,
and looked like she was ready to go until dawn.
She yelled something about animal rights,
and protectin' the critters and their unfair plight.
He was getting desperate and wanted to leave,
she was pointin' at the horns and startin' to grieve.
After two more shots she was settlin' down,
she was beginning to mumble and stagger around.
That was his clue to slip out into the night,
he saddled up his horse for the downhill flight.
Before leaving he put a note on the door,
saying follow the trail to the valley floor.

The going's not easy and pretty slow,
but it will return you safely to the ranch below.

As he rode down the hill and into the night,
he wondered how long she would keep up the fight.
It was a pretty close call as he looked back,
and was glad it happened now instead of after-the-fact.
He got to thinkin' that it turned out like it should,
maybe, herdin' cattle for a livin' is pretty damn good.

There are times of the year when our group actually does something else for outdoor entertainment other than hunting. However, even when we play a round of golf, the hunting experience comes in handy to help hunters out that are trying another sport.

TIME OUT

I have this friend who's known for his hunting skills,
he can make long shots and animals fall at his will.
He has many trophies on the walls in his house,
and we hear great stories when we visit him and his spouse.
"That on there, as he points to a rack,
was almost straight up, I had to lay on my back."
"But when I shot he tumbled down to me,
and now I have him for all to see."
He could go on for hours telling his tales,
of hunting down elk on high mountain trails.
We would sit there in awe as we looked around the room,
thinking that the first day of hunting couldn't come any too
soon.
But hunting season was a long way off,
so I suggested to my friend, "let's play some golf."
We packed up our gear and headed for the "green,"
the bag for his clubs was unusually large it seemed.

When it was our turn to tee off on "number one,"
I watched my friend and knew the fun had begun.
He pulled his range-finder out, checked the distance to the
      hole,
chambered a ball on the tee, and let one go.
"Now that was a shot," as he turned to me with glee,
I watched the ball slice then bounce back from a tree.

A couple of holes later and well into our game,
my friend was down four strokes and he started to complain.

"My eyes are blurring when I look at the ball,
and my shoulder hurts when the club starts to fall."
But I knew his real problem, health it was not,
he needed an incentive to focus in on his shot.
I jumped into the cart and raced up ahead,
upon the flag of the hole, I drew an elks head.

The antlers were big and met Boone and Crockett size,
and when I returned I could see the gleam in his eyes.
He had a 6X scope and was scanning forward and back,
when the cross-hairs landed upon the big bull's rack.
"He said, I see it now, it's 300 yards up ahead,
and with one shot I can take it, it will soon be dead."
He drove the green and it was into the sun,
aiming at the "bull" he made a hole in one.
It was down-hill for me the rest of the game,
I knew that golfing with my friend would never be the same.

And now when we go out hunting in the fall,
he'll brag about the new trophy hanging on his wall.
It's a little yellow flag with a picture of a bull elk,
it wasn't just luck, "it was all skill," he felt.
So if you see a golf course with elk antlers on the flags,
watch for my friend with a 6X scope in his bag.
He'll talk about magnums and 180 grains
and he'll approach a green, as if he were hunting game.
And God help you if you bet, even if it's for fun,
if there's elk horns on the flag, he'll make a hole-in-one.

If you ever see this next character out there while you're hunting, get as much distance as possible between you and him as fast as possible. Anybody with a high-powered rifle and having problems like that guy is a bad combination.

THE PURPLE BUCK

I knew that I'd had too much to drink,
when I lifted my head up from the sink.
I staggered out the door to get in my truck,
and ran head-long into the Purple Buck.

He was six feet tall to the top of his back,
teeth like a bear and daggers for a rack.
He didn't look friendly he just looked mean,
and started chasing me around my drivin' machine.

I was screamin' and yellin' and cryin' for help,
when his horns hit my rear I started to yelp.
He was bearin' down upon me with all of his might,
All I wanted to do, was run not fight.

But there was no where to go or to get away,
I had to face this foe who didn't want to play.
I pulled out my knife in an attempt to fight,
my body was weary, and shakin' with fright.

I was swingin' my knife to fend off those horns,
I was prayin' to the lord; I was soundin' forlorn.
"Lord get him away, this demon deer,"
"I'll swear off of whiskey, wine and beer."
"I'll do anything you ask of me,
and become a saint for the world to see."

His charge was straight and he hit my back,
I fell to the ground and everything went black.
The world started swirling and I heard a sound,
I lifted my head and turned around.

"Get to hell up from there," she yelled at me,
"you're a miserable sight for the world to see."
It wasn't an angel, it was my wife instead,
I was happy and grinnin" 'cause I knew I wasn't dead.

And now when I go huntin' in the fall of the year,
I drink water and pop, no more whiskey and beer.
But when I'm alone I still have this fear,
that again I may run into, that purple deer.

Some guys just have a knack for getting themselves into a pressure situation. This next poem pretty much describes one of those times.

SNEAKIN'

We were sitting in camp in the middle of the day,
when we spotted three bucks a long way away.
There was no cover for a thousand yards,
and one of the bucks had antlers quite large.

There was no chance to get close to that buck,
even if we had extremely good luck.
But one man in the crowd, got that gleam in his eyes.
He was known as Hans, one heck of a nice guy.

He was taller than most with a raw-bone frame,
and sneaking up on deer was his claim to fame.
He was like a chameleon when going through the brush.
and across open clearing he'd close in a rush.

He checked out the wind and circled in a direction,
it gave him the advantage after making the correction.
We watched and waited as he moved up the hill,
and got closer and closer to his future kill.

One buck looked up while Hans was in the open,
Hans froze in his tracks while the buck was a scopin'.
Satisfied that all he saw was a juniper tree,
and again started to eat, rather than to flee.

Then Hans got down on his hands and knees,
and was hidden by the grass, there were no more trees.
Inch by inch he crawled up the hill,
he moved with great stealth and extremely good skill.

Then the worst that could happen,
in this game of high stakes,
laid coiled three feet ahead—a rattlesnake!

Hans pulled out his knife, while starring at the snake,
he knew this had to be done with no mistakes.
Anticipating it's move he held the knife out ahead,
when the snake jumped toward him, it cut off it's own head.

This was all done with very little sound,
and the deer up the hill hadn't looked around.
He continued his course, crawling up toward the deer.
We were watching, anxiously, it seemed like a year.

Hans felt everyone's eyes on his back they did burn,
he could hear the jeers of failure when he returned.
Instead of making him nervous it gave him resolve,
and with the squeeze of the trigger, he'd watch the buck fall.

The distance now short their eyes would meet,
he slowly came up and stood on his feet.
With his gun to his shoulder, he took aim and fired,
his body was shakin' and his nerves were "wired."

He took a deep breath and looked up ahead,
he had made a good shot, the buck lay dead.
We all cheered from camp when he made his shot,
and knew this was the best of a super great stalk.

They will speak of him in the future, around the camp fire,
and the story will get better with each succeeding liar.
They'll say out hunting he's an ordinary walker,
but put him on a deer's track, he becomes Hans the Stalker.

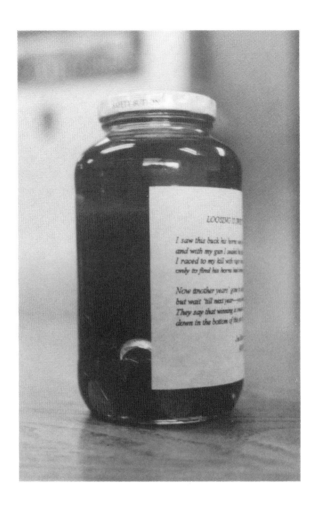

I started writing poems last year after losing a bet to a good friend. This year, another bet was made with another good friend. After realizing failure two years in a row, losing has begun to take its effect on my mind. Last year my loss of the bet was counteracted by one hell of a good shot. However, this year I couldn't come up with any viable explanation as to why I had come home with a relatively small buck. Therefore, my motive in the method that I paid off my bet was a little on the mischievous side. God, it was great!

LOSING IS SWEET

I saw this buck his horns were great,
and with my gun I sealed his fate.
I raced to my kill with vigor and spunk,
only to find his horns had shrunk.
Now another years' gone by and I've lost another bet,
but wait 'till next year—you haven't seen nothin' yet.
They say that winning is sweet, so here's your money,
down in the bottom of this jar of honey!

HUNTER'S PRAYER

Dear Lord in heaven I stand here today,
in hopes that you will listen to what I say.
It's been a good life, but I'm getting up in years,
and each day is a blessing as my time gets nearer.
But one thing stands out most of all,
is giving me the gift of hunting in the fall.

So lord I'm asking when I get to your gate,
that I can bring my rifle, If heaven is my fate,
and another thing, if it's not asking too much,
having big bucks to hunt, would give it a nice touch.

ORDER FORM

To order additional copies of
Horns, Guns and Hunters,
send a check or money order
for $8.95 plus 3.00 shipping and handling
to:

6080 MILLER Book Order
~~6767 Hess Road~~
Mt. Hood-Parkdale, OR 97041